GEMS
NATURE'S JEWELS

AMBER

By Michael Rajczak

Gareth Stevens
PUBLISHING

Please visit our website, www.garethstevens.com. For a free color catalog of all our high-quality books, call toll free 1-800-542-2595 or fax 1-877-542-2596.

Library of Congress Cataloging-in-Publication Data

Rajczak, Michael.
Amber / by Michael Rajczak.
p. cm. — (Gems: nature's jewels)
Includes index.
ISBN 978-1-4824-2852-0 (pbk.)
ISBN 978-1-4824-2853-7 (6 pack)
ISBN 978-1-4824-2854-4 (library binding)
1. Precious stones — Juvenile literature. 2. Fossils — Juvenile literature.I. Rajczak, Michael. II. Title.
QE392.R35 2016
553.8—d23

First Edition

Published in 2016 by
Gareth Stevens Publishing
111 East 14th Street, Suite 349
New York, NY 10003

Copyright © 2016 Gareth Stevens Publishing

Designer: Andrea Davison-Bartolotta
Editor: Kristen Rajczak

Photo credits: Cover, p. 1 Damaratskaya Alena/Shutterstock.com; p. 5 orangecrush/Shutterstock.com; p. 7 (main) Igor Boldyrev/Shutterstock.com; p. 7 (inset) Andy38/Shutterstock.com; p. 8 (far left) humbak/Shutterstock.com; p. 8 (left middle) cristi180884/Shutterstock.com; p. 8 (right middle) Renewer/Shutterstock.com; p. 8 (far right) canismaior/Shutterstock.com; p. 9 Vladimir Sazonov/Shutterstock.com; p. 11 Paul Zahl/National Geographic/Getty Images; pp. 12–13 MyLoupe/UIG/Getty Images; p. 14 Galyna Andrushko/Shutterstock.com; p. 15 (main) ChinellatoPhoto/Shutterstock.com; p. 15 (inset) Baciu/Shutterstock.com; p. 16 DEA/G. Dagli Orti/Getty Images; p. 17 DEA Picture Library/Getty Images; p. 18 skyfish/Shutterstock.com; p. 19 jeanyfan/Wikimedia Commons; p. 20 © iStockphoto.com/ProArtWork; p. 21 Mattz90/Shutterstock.com.

Printed in the United States of America

CPSIA compliance information: Batch #CS15GS: For further information contact Gareth Stevens, New York, New York at 1-800-542-2595.

Contents

Words in the glossary appear in **bold** type the first time they are used in the text.

What Is Amber?

Amber is a fossil. A fossil is the hardened remains or marks of a plant or animal from long ago. Amber is also a gem!

Amber began as resin, a sticky matter that comes from trees. This resin hardened, and once the tree died, was later buried in soil, sand, and other matter, called sediment. Over time, great heat and **pressure** turned the hardened resin into amber. Not all trees make resin that can become amber. Some hardened pieces of resin break down too quickly to fossilize.

Be a Gem Genius!

A tree produces resin to take care of any harm that comes to it, such as a branch breaking off. It's like a **bandage**, covering the place that's been harmed and hardening.

A gem is a stone that's cut, polished, and worth money. Unlike other gems, amber isn't made of minerals, or the matter that forms rocks.

Where Is Amber Found?

Amber can be found all over the world. The largest **deposits** of amber in the world are on the shore of the Baltic Sea in northern Europe. The amber there is about 35 to 60 million years old! Amber is found in Germany, Poland, and Russia. Indonesia and Burma in southeastern Asia are also rich sources of amber.

The amber found in the Dominican Republic is younger than Baltic amber. It formed about 15 to 20 million years ago!

Be a Gem Genius!

The sediment in which hardened tree resin was buried often became sandstone. It's in this kind of rock that amber may be found.

Most of the world's amber comes from a mine, or a place where stone or gems are dug up, in Kaliningrad, Russia. Mining uncovers amber in North America and Asia as well.

Baltic Sea

What Does Amber Look Like?

Amber is often transparent, meaning it's easy to see through. However, some amber is cloudy looking or completely **opaque** because of air bubbles trapped in the gem. Even clear amber sometimes has air bubbles you can see!

Amber comes in many different sizes and shapes, some smaller than a grain of sand and some heavier than 8 pounds (3.6 kg)! It may form in teardrop shapes or tall, thin rods. Smooth, pebble-like amber can be found on beaches and coasts.

Transparent amber gems are often more **valuable** than those that are a bit cloudy.

So Colorful

When most people think of amber, they picture many different shades of yellow and brown. That's often Baltic amber. But beautiful amber of other colors is found in Indonesia. Called Sumatra amber, it's valuable because it often contains different colors, including navy blue and pale green. The Dominican Republic is a rich source of amber that looks blue!

Bone amber gets its name from its milky white appearance. Red amber is sometimes called cherry amber. There's also black amber known as jet.

Be a Gem Genius!

If you shine a light through blue amber from the Dominican Republic, you'll see a reddish-brown or honey color.

Because "amber" is the name of a color, it's easy to think the gem of the same name only comes in that color! This blue amber shows another beautiful color amber gems can be.

Handle with Care

Amber is very soft compared to gems like diamonds and rubies. It's between 1 and 3 out of 10 on the Mohs scale of mineral hardness! That means it's easily scratched. Amber is also brittle, or easily broken.

Though amber often has a nice **luster**, oxygen in the air may cause the gem to get darker in color. Its outer layer may start to look dull and form a crust. This can begin to happen after just 10 or 20 years.

Be a Gem Genius!

Amber can be man-made. You can tell a piece of natural amber by seeing if it floats in salt water.

Here is a piece of raw amber that needs to be polished and cut before being used for **jewelry**.

Secrets Inside

Unlike other gems, **inclusions** in amber often make it more valuable. Sometimes bugs or other matter gets trapped in the tree resin. When the resin fossilizes into amber, the bug inside is perfectly **preserved**. Each piece of amber that contains a bug can tell scientists something about the past, such as what the weather was like when the bug was trapped.

Because no two pieces of amber are alike, inclusions like these are very valuable. Flies, gnats, spiders, and grasshoppers have been found caught in amber.

The book and movie *Jurassic Park* were based on the idea that dinosaur blood had been found inside a mosquito that had been preserved in amber.

Bugs were often caught in amber because they were drawn by the sweet smell of the tree resin—and trapped!

Cool Amber in History

Amber may be the oldest **semiprecious** gem. It's one of the first products ancient people traveled long distances to trade. By the first century AD, amber was wanted so badly by the ancient Romans that they created a trade route just so they could get the beautiful gems.

During the **Middle Ages** in Europe, amber was used to make beautiful **rosaries**. It was so valued that those in charge of amber trade punished anyone found collecting the gem for themselves!

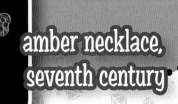

amber necklace, seventh century

This amber cameo of Emperor Rudolf II comes from the early 17th century. A cameo is a kind of jewelry with something carved, or cut, into the main stone.

17

Mystical Amber

During the Middle Ages, a handful of amber meant you were wealthy! But there were many ancient beliefs about amber that gave it a different kind of value.

Wearing amber was once thought to be a way to keep safe or to help heal illness. People used to bury amber beneath their home for good luck. Placing amber with a person who died was thought to help him or her on the journey to the afterlife.

Be a Gem Genius!

Some ancient tribes thought pieces of amber were bits of the sun that fell from the sky!

In 1979, the building of a room made of amber began in Russia. It was a re-creation of an amber room built in the 1700s that was stolen by the Germans during World War II (1939–1945).

Making Amber Jewelry

Today, amber is used to make necklaces, bracelets, earrings, and rings. To clean natural amber and clear any cloudiness, the gem is sometimes placed in hot oil or heated in a special oven. Jewelers then polish and cut the amber into a shape.

Some people even have jewelry with ancient bugs or leaves in them! Jewelers who make these pieces try to cut the amber to show off these inclusions the best they can. Would you like amber jewelry like this?

How Amber Gems Are Made

a tree produces resin → resin hardens → hardened resin is buried in sediment → heat and pressure fossilize the resin into amber → amber is polished and shaped into gems

21

Glossary

bandage: a piece of cloth or other material used to cover a wound

deposit: an amount of a mineral in the ground that built up over a period of time

inclusion: a piece of matter caught inside a gem

jewelry: pieces of metal, often holding gems, worn on the body

luster: the glow created by reflected light

Middle Ages: a time in European history from about 500 to about 1500

opaque: unable to be seen through

polish: to make something smooth and shiny by rubbing it with a soft cloth

preserve: to keep something in its original state

pressure: a force that pushes on something else

rosary: a string of beads used to represent a series of prayers

semiprecious: describing stones that are often used as gems but aren't the most valuable gems

valuable: worth a lot of money

For More Information

Books

Hyde, Natalie. *Plant Fossils.* New York, NY: Crabtree Publishing Company, 2014.

Ross, Andrew. *Amber: The National Time Capsule.* Buffalo, NY: Firefly Books, 2010.

VanVoorst, Jenny Fretland. *Gems.* Minneapolis, MN: Core Library, 2015.

Websites

Amber
gemkids.gia.edu/gem/amber
Read more about amber's history, colors, and formation here.

How Amber Forms
www.bbc.co.uk/programmes/p00ckj8s
Watch a BBC video about how amber forms.

Index